Mouth To

A Prophetic Interpretation

31 Day Words of Life

Devotional Journal

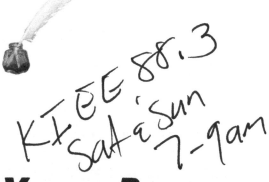

KIEE 88.3
Sat & Sun
7-9am

Marlice Young-Dugas

331-349-9190

Mouth to Mouth - A Prophetic Interpretation
31 Day Words of Life Devotional Journal
Marlice Young-Dugas

Printed in the United States of America

ISBN - 10: 0692140921   ISBN – 13: 978-
0692140925

Unless otherwise indicated, all bible quotations are taken from the NLT version of the bible.

Developmental Editing by Nedra Epps, Vision Heirs Publishing and Consulting

Cover design by Marlice Young-Dugas and Lorna Abercrombie Landry (Art Work)

Published by CreateSpace: an Amazon Company

Dedication

When you are passionate about something, that passion gives you the energy necessary to be able to do the very thing you were created and put on this earth to do. From my hidden treasury and unseen passion came this book, which is dedicated to my family, my friends, and those who have been called to serve alongside me in the kingdom.

I would like to take this moment and personally thank you for your sacrifice in prayer, for your tears, and for your willingness to do life with me even in the most difficult moments of my life. Words cannot express how grateful I am for your encouragement during this process, especially when I could not see the end. But you constantly reminded me of what was possible.

This work is also dedicated to every person who feels the call to something greater; but you don't have the means, or you do not quite know how to express what you are feeling. I dedicate this work to you. Never be afraid to use your voice. Don't be afraid to speak your truth. The spirit of Christ is in you.

Finally, I dedicate this work back to the Father, the One who has given me the gift, ability and strength to complete this love command all the way to the end.

Again, I extend a heartfelt thank you to all.

Marlice

Table of Contents

Table of Contents continued ...

Foreword

As a covenant, five-fold, kingdom servant, Marlice Young-Dugas has compiled this book of daily readings to stir the body of Christ. It is designed to lift individuals out of their lethargy, their woundedness, and their ignorance–to become the spiritual warriors they were made to be–to shake them out of mere mental assent and into bold action. This is not a collection of sweet platitudes, but a call for "the dry bones" to arise as God's end time army.

Ignorance (lack of spiritual understanding) plagues the church in this country. Our arch enemy, the devil, has labored feverishly over the years to deceive and, thereby, rob us of our God given identity and purpose. This has resulted in a church that does not know who they really are. Although we have been created to be His overcoming co-workers (1 Corinthians 3:9), reconciling the world back to Him (2 Corinthians 5:19-20), many have become passive and complacent, relying totally on their own understanding. Spiritual warfare rages, and the body of Christ flounders, unable or unwilling to rise up in the face of daily demonic attacks. God's army can barely stand, unsure how to "get their act together."

Obviously, the body of Christ needs a makeover. Some need healing, some need training, and all need to truly understand the call for them to "push back the gates of hell" (Matthew 16:18). All have to know without a doubt that they were sent just as Jesus was sent (John 17:18-20).

The primary solution for all these problems is for people to get to know their Maker — the One who loves them so much, He sent His son to lay down His life for them. He knows them better than they know themselves. They need to know without question that they are fearfully and wonderfully made (Psalms139:13-16) and specially designed for the reason for which they were sent (Ephesians 2:10).

Our primary endeavor should, therefore, be to get to intimately know our Father, so that He has our ear, and we will know His will for us each day. Then we will truly be able to be His ambassadors, the actual extension of His will, moving in His strength and power (Ephesians 6:10).

Marlice, a truly committed Kingdom servant, has been an example of this in her own life. Out of the ashes of adversity, Marlice has arisen to lay claim to the inheritance that is rightfully hers. She has experienced and overcome the traumas and pitfalls of life. She saw them as challenges, overcoming rather than folding like a cheap suitcase. Having "been there and done that," she is in a position to enlighten and encourage those who have yet to figure out how to rise up, rather than go under.

The following pages will build confidence and instill a true understanding of purpose and destiny to needy readers. This book will be a worthy addition to your personal library and will daily feed and build up your spirit.

Apostle Bruce Gunkle
City of Refuge Christian Fellowship
San Antonio, Texas

MOUTH TO MOUTH

C (CHRIST'S) P (PERFECT) R (REDEMPTION)

He breathed into man the breath of life, and man
became a living soul

Genesis 2:7

Revive Me According to Your Word —Psalm 119:25

It is amazing when we begin to think of mankind's response to the spoken word of God. There are so many instances recorded of God's word being the guidelines for life. The miraculous begins when the Holy Spirit uses our hearts as tablets to express the mind and will of the Father at a given moment in time. It reminds us that He still speaks to the spirit of a man who has a longing to be betrothed and wooed by the essence of His love. How incredible the yielded heart that yearns for the expression of grace, only to be unveiled daily as we are reminded of the way we are drawn close to Him by the completed work of the cross. Jesus paid the price, so we can be near our Abba once more. I call it CPR or Christ's Perfect Redemption, whereby through His Words He makes us alive again.

Mouth to Mouth is a journal of divine expressions flowing from my heart's surrender to Christ in love. To me, His voice resuscitates daily. It is my hope that the writings will revive, renew, and restore you to life again. Mouth to mouth ... I believe He still speaks.

Forever His Servant,
Marlice Young-Dugas

Day 1

Revive me by your word, your word is life.
Psalm 119:25

I am close to death. Give me a new life as you promised.
Psalm 119:25
GOD'S WORD® Translation (©1995)

mouth to mouth resuscitation:

an emergency procedure consisting of external cardiac massage and artificial respiration; the first treatment for a person who has collapsed and has no pulse and has stopped breathing; attempts to restore circulation of the blood and prevent death or brain damage due to lack of oxygen

Let Me Resuscitate You

In this world of confusion, the only thing you must rely on is Me. As you draw close to Me, I will draw close to you. I see the condition of your soul. I see you are dying spiritually. Let Me take you away. There is still so much for you to learn. There is a depth to Me that has been hidden from all of creation. It is revealed to those who search for Me with all their hearts.

You say, "I am so tired." I say, "I knew you would get to this point even before the womb of your mother." I have watched you day after day functioning in your own strength. I have watched you trying to put all the pieces together. I have watched you, in a state of confusion, so desperately creating ritualistic acts of performance. As an actor who performs as a means to sustain his life, so you have performed to the point that your soul is weak.

Come today, my child, and allow Me to give you mouth to mouth. Let Me resuscitate you. Let Me speak a word today to redeem your soul. Sit quietly for a moment, and I will teach you what I have so desired to teach you all along. What would I teach you today as I resuscitate you? I would teach you that I am your safe place; I am your protection; I am your shelter.

Do not be afraid to let Me see that you are in a vulnerable place. Come on, my child—be real. I will not turn away. Please allow Me to help you today. I can plainly see that you are defenseless; you are helpless; your soul is opened and exposed; and you are in danger and at risk of becoming an open target for the enemy.

What I am saying is, you are in a current state of weakness. But I have declared already—when you are weak, I am strong. Learn today in your state of spiritual anemia that My blood is flushing out the weaknesses of your soul. Receive my C.P.R.! I declare to you today that for every place of inadequacy, My grace is sufficient. Breathe, child, breathe.

Mouth to mouth ... let Me resuscitate you.

Prayer

Father, I thank you today that I can breathe knowing that Your strength is made perfect in my weakness. Thank You for reviving me by the power of Your word. I admit that I have functioned in my own strength, but I release all self performance, and I stand back today and allow the Holy Spirit to lead me along peaceful streams, in Jesus' Name, Amen.

Prophetic Declaration

I declare that I am resuscitated by the power of Your word. I have spoken it! I decree it! It is so, NOW!

Notes

Day 2

Give the kiss of life to Me as I behold your face.
Song of Solomon 1:2a

mouth to mouth resuscitation (mouth′tə-mouth′):
A technique used to resuscitate a person who has stopped breathing, in which the rescuer presses his or her mouth against the mouth of the victim and, allowing for passive exhalation, forces air into the lungs at intervals of several seconds.

kiss of life:
artificial respiration by the mouth-to-mouth method

Intimacy Is Required

I am calling you into a life of purity. Purity is the spiritual center of your life — the actions, the motives of your heart. When purity is birthed forth from your womb it brings Me great delight. It births intimacy. Intimacy with Me is birthed from your willingness to be separated unto Me. At this place in your walk with Me, I must become your priority. Intimacy with Me is absolutely necessary.

As you behold My face today, I will kiss you with the kiss of life. Kissing is a signification of My love, as well as a sign of heartfelt intimacy. As I wooed Job out of his distress, so will I do for you. Allow Me to love you to a place of being all that I have created you to be. It is a place of being cleansed, being whole, being right—just being who I have created you to be.

When I love, I love you right. When you are right, then, and only then, are you pure in heart and prepared for intimacy— blameless in who I created you to be; having a desire to please Me in all things.

Today intimacy is rare. It is not only a word, but it's a lifestyle. I said that the pure in heart would have access to Me. Drop all that has taken your attention, and give Me your heart once again. If you could only imagine how much I love you. If you could only imagine.

Today I give to you the kiss of life as Solomon offered. As you look to me, as you behold me, I will speak to you gently. It is the pure in heart that I said will see Me. Run to Me. I am waiting to woo you away from all that distracts you and produces an eternal disruption which takes you away from purpose.

Mouth to mouth ... intimacy with Me is key in this season.

Prayer

Father, today I come to you asking that you draw me close to You. It is intimacy that I desire today. I ask You to woo me out of all that hinders my divine purpose, in Jesus Name, Amen.

Prophetic Declaration

I declare that intimacy is my portion as I am wooed by the Love of God. I have spoken it! I decree it! It is so, NOW!

Notes

Day 3

That is why I'm going to win her back. I will lead her into the desert. I will speak tenderly to her.

Hosea 2:14
GOD'S WORD® Translation (©1995)

resuscitation:

the act of reviving a person and returning them to consciousness; "although he was apparently drowned, resuscitation was accomplished by artificial respiration"

I am Winning You Back

Be still and know that I am God! I will be exalted in your life. I know you can't figure out what I am doing in your life; but just wait and see that you will come into the fullness of everything I have spoken. My plans will begin to unfold, and you will understand.

I've told you before and, now, I speak again. You will see. Things are opening up and being made known before your eyes! Seek me with all your heart, mind, and soul. You must come before me in prayer and wait silently for instructions. I will breathe new life into you. There is a course correction and course direction that I will reveal to you in this season. It will cause you to rise out of the prostration of your flesh to move forward in faith to bring life to others.

Are you prepared for this? You will see things that you have never seen before. You will hear things you have never heard. You are getting ready to go places that you have never gone. Please, I ask you, submit to the power of My Word. My word is My will for your life. All things at this very moment, as I breathe into the existence of your very being, are working out for good. Will you trust Me? I am speaking tenderly to you. Yes, it has been a desert experience. Only know that I am in charge of everything.

This is a season where you enter into total agreement with Me, and I become your only reason for being. Trust me, my love, trust me. Do not be afraid of what you cannot see.

Remember my child; it is all up to Me. You have suffered enough. I have come to win you back. Feel the wind of My spirit, which is My breath. I am breathing into you right as this very moment, so take it in. My glory is surrounding you. I am restoring you to consciousness. Rise now and enter your place to become a partaker of My divine nature. This will enable you to inherit all the promises that have been spoken over your life. Relax, I am absolutely in control. Inhale! Exhale! Don't hold on! Take in My word! It's time to live.

Mouth to mouth ... you are a winner!

Prayer

Father, I thank You that You are absolutely in control of every detail of my life. I thank You that my desert experiences have made me stronger. I ask You to restore me in the spirit of my mind so that I can be consciously aware of Your presence. I
ask You to breathe life into me and cause me to live for
Your glory, in Jesus' Name, Amen.

Prophetic Declaration

I declare that I am restored to spiritual consciousness, and the wind of God's spirit blows through my soul. I have spoken it! I decree it! It is so, NOW!

Notes

Day 4

He is wooing you from the jaws of distress to a spacious place free from restriction, to the comfort of your table laden with choice food.

Job 36:16
New International Version

wooed, woo·ing, woos:
To seek the affection of with intent to romance

I AM Wooing You!!

This is your season for divine intervention. You have been faithful over little, so now I am going to make you ruler over much. Doors of opportunity are opening for you. Don't worry about anything, because the Word has already settled everything.

Arise in My Glory and move forward in My anointing. Things that have held you bound for years will now release you and let you go. It is called the wooing process. My love will draw you into My purpose. Remember when I spoke to Lazarus who had been bound in grave clothes and said, "Loose that man and let him go." He was wooed out of his distress. I am speaking this to you today. Don't forget the woman with the issue of blood when I spoke to her and said, "Woman, you are loosed from your infirmity." In other words, I was telling her that she was released from her instabilities, feebleness, imperfections, and weaknesses. She was wooed out of her distress.

Are you any different? I beg to differ. The answer is NO. I am the same yesterday, today, and forevermore. Your shackles are breaking, and strongholds are being pulled down. It is ... simply by the sound of My voice. My voice speaks authoritatively today in Love.

Am I not still the Lord of My servants? I am still moved with compassion. I am still forgiving and releasing you from your spiritual debts – and yes, I am still loosing My people. It's time to receive your deliverance by faith and enter into your inheritance.

Do you feel the wooing? You have been chosen for this time. I, the Lord, declare to you that I am arising in Zion and having mercy upon you; for it is the set time to favor you. Yes, the set time has come. I am the perfecter of all things and have already perfected that which concerns you. Be expecting the unexpected. I mean, just look for crazy (out of the ordinary, but all good) things to start happening to you this day. I declare and decree it for you. I agree with you. Will you agree with Me? It is bigger than what you can see and greater than what you know. Look for My miracles today!

Mouth to mouth ... I AM wooing you into a season of better things.

Prayer

Father, I thank You today that you are wooing me out of my distresses into greater things. I receive deliverance today in every area of my life, in Jesus' Name, Amen.

Prophetic Declaration

I declare that I have divine favor from God, and my set time of favor is now. I have spoken it! I decree it! It is so, NOW!

Notes

Day 5

For our light affliction, which is but for a moment, is working for us a far more exceeding and eternal weight of glory, while we do not look at the things which are seen, but at the things which are not seen. For the things which are seen are temporary, but the things which are not seen are eternal.
2 Corinthians 4:17
New King James Version

Then Hezekiah and all the people rejoiced over what God had prepared for the people, because the thing came about suddenly.
2 Chronicles 29:36
New American Standard Bible

sudden:

happening without warning; unforeseen; very quickly and unexpectedly

The Season for Suddenly

Remember when Paul went to the Church of Corinth, and I used him to remind them that the trials they were facing were temporary. Then he proceeded to tell them, if they found themselves in the midst of suffering, they must understand that sometimes you suffer according to the will of God.

I have invested so much on the inside of you. I know you will allow patience to have her perfect work through you; and I promise, you will come out victoriously–suddenly. I need you to pay attention closely to your surroundings and watch. You see, my child, you could be on your way to the grocery store and then– suddenly. You could be getting ready to go to bed and then– suddenly.

Paul encouraged my children, even back then, that the adversities were only temporary and not worthy to be compared to the Glory that I was getting ready to reveal in their lives. My Glory has a way of just showing up suddenly. Again, remember, the Red Sea opened up suddenly. Paul and Silas were in jail, and the prison doors opened suddenly. On the third day, Jesus rose ... how? Suddenly. Mary and Martha thought that their brother was dead. But, what? Suddenly, I spoke the Word and said, "Lazarus come forth," and immediately the grave clothes fell off—suddenly. The woman with the issue of blood was healed—suddenly. Esther, when she went before the king, delivered the nation of Israel—suddenly. I sent a ram in the bush for Abraham—suddenly.

Now, are you any different from the rest? Know that your breakthrough will come—suddenly. Expect it. My goodness will show up on your behalf—suddenly. This is your season for a "Vicarious Victory." This means that My Son, Jesus, won the fight, and you get the prize. How? Suddenly. Your suddenly is today. Look for it and expect it.

Mouth to mouth ... this is your season for suddenly!

Prayer

Father, I have not always allowed patience to work in me. Help me to let patience have its perfect work in me, so I will not be lacking in any good thing You have for me. I receive victory and every intentional suddenly in my life, in Jesus' name, Amen.

Prophetic Declaration

I declare the suddenlies of God are sweeping me off my feet today with favor, joy, strength and multiplied goodness. I have spoken it! I decree it! It is so, NOW!

Notes

Day 6

The Lord [is] good unto them that wait for him, to the soul [that] seeketh Him.
Lamentations 3:25
King James Version

seek:
to search for (someone or something): to try to find (someone or something)

What Are You Seeking?

What are you seeking today? Do you seek for earthly things in this life to satisfy you? Do you seek for the opinions of people to satisfy you? Do you seek after fleshly appetites to satisfy you? Do you seek positions and titles to satisfy you? What are you seeking today to make you satisfied?

Did I not say in My Word that if you would seek first MY Kingdom, then you would never come up short? For the Kingdom is not a physical place – it is MY joy; it is MY peace; and it is MY ability to live right, do right and be right in this treacherous world.

Many times, you remain so worldly minded, you totally miss out on your God given "Kingdom Assignment." You continuously look for things, stuff, and people to fill the voids you may be experiencing. I encourage you to seek Me today.

Allow Me to impart an anointing that will completely destroy and remove every burden and yoke in your life. This is an anointing to rise above your mess and move you into your message; an anointing to release you out of your Egypt into your promised land; an anointing to place you on top. It is an anointing that will satisfy every soul desire and put your flesh to rest in order to enter into My best.

Seek ME today! Only I can satisfy. Remember, heaven and earth will pass away; but My word will always remain. As you seek Me you will find me. You can find Me in my Word. You can listen for Me in a song. You can feel Me in the wind. You can see Me clearly in others. I am not far away. I am ALWAYS near. I AM the only one who can satisfy you; and in seeking Me, you will not walk away empty.

Let's make a commitment today to allow ME, "Jesus" only, to satisfy every void in your life. My spirit is waiting. Commune with Him today. Don't hold back. Be blessed today, My Child. Simply, be blessed.

Mouth to mouth ... what are you seeking?

Prayer

Father, today I commit to seeking You and only You. I thank You for replenishing every dry area of my life. Breathe fresh breath into me, so I can live again, in Jesus' name, Amen.

Prophetic Declaration

I declare as I seek God, I will be anointed to live on top. I have spoken it! I decree it! It is so, NOW!

Notes

Day 7

For many are called, but few [are] chosen.
Matthew 22:14
King James Version

use:

take, hold, or deploy (something) as a means of accomplishing a purpose or achieving a result;

I Want to Use You

You will speak My words of truth. Say only what I tell you to say. I will give you clear insight, and you will know exactly what I am doing. Do not be afraid of the terror that you may be facing in the world at this present moment. It is temporary. In a moment I will come to your defense and intervene on your behalf. You have nothing to lose, only much to gain.

Be diligent in your commitment to Me. Continue to let Me mold you and shape your character. I *need* you to be diligent and keep a pure heart. *Please* allow Me to mold you and shape you, because I want to use you. It is MY image that I am looking for, not any of your preconceived ideas. There is so much to be done in the earth, and I want to do it through you.

Doors of opportunity are opening that will give you a chance to be a witness. Don't be afraid of what is coming ahead. Be steadfast, and I will lead you step by step. There is much to be revealed. Listen attentively for My voice in the quiet of the night, and I will speak to you.

Oh, how much I have in store for you! Forget your past and move on. Why sit here and die? This is no time for regrets; no time to reminiscence; no more time to nurse or rehearse the wounds of your past. Get up, stand on your feet, and move on!

I desire to launch you into the deep. You know that deep calls unto deep. In order to embrace the deeper things of the kingdom, you must be willing to die to your own selfish desires. Do not use anything that would be familiar to you. I am referring to your own equipment. I mean precisely the things that you have conjured up in the flesh yet call it the spirit. The things you have created for yourself, yet call it Me. These things keep you in your comfort zone, because you are comfortable with yourself.

Today, will you step out with a sacrifice? Give Me your best. What do you have to lose? Nothing. You only have My Kingdom to gain. I have hidden treasures in secret places waiting to be discovered by you. This is a call to service—true service. I really want to use you! Step out, beloved! You have what it takes. You are ready.

Mouth to mouth ... I want to use you.

Prayer

Father, today I see that You have a plan for my life; and it is far beyond what I can imagine. I am yielded to you today. Despite what I may be feeling, I lay aside all flesh that I may receive treasures in secret places, in Jesus' Name, Amen.

Prophetic Declaration

I declare today that God is using me, and all hidden treasures are mine. I have spoken it! I decree it! It is so, NOW!

Notes

_____

_____

_____

_____

_____

_____

_____

_____

_____

_____

_____

_____

_____

Day 8

[Hagar] gave this name to the Lord who spoke to her: You are the
God who sees me
Genesis 16:13a
New International Version

see:
perceive with the eyes; discern visually.

I See You!

I know this has been a difficult season, but I see you. You have labored to no end. I sit back and watch you day after day struggling to do things in your own effort. I want you to know I see you. I see your uprising. I see your outgoing. I see your outcome. I see your heart. I see your situation. I see you. I See you. I SEE you.

My eyes are like x-ray vision seeing the inner most parts of your being. I see the healing that needs to take place in your soul. Do not continue to fight against the plans I have so perfectly aligned for your life. I see all your hopes and dreams. I see all your disappointment and pain. I see your willingness to help; and oft times you are rejected and pushed away. I see your moments of confusion. I see you.

But from My viewpoint, I need you to see yourself. I need you to see that you are more than a conqueror. I need you to see that all your sufficiency is from Me. I need you to see that all is provided in Me. I need you to see that all is well in Me. I need you to gain an eternal perspective.

Today I say, struggle no more with futile projects. I am looking for fruitfulness in everything you do from this day forward.

Mouth to mouth ... I see you.

Prayer

Father, I ask You to see into the deepest parts of my heart and take away anything that hinders me from my full potential of becoming all You have created me to be, in Jesus' Name, Amen.

Prophetic Declaration

I declare I see me as God sees me. I have spoken it! I decree it! It is so, NOW!

Notes

Day 9

*But as for me, to draw near to God is good; I have put my hope in the
LORD GOD, that I may declare all thy works.*
Psalm 73:28
Jubilee Bible 2000

Draw:
to move (as a covering) over or to one side

911 – Draw Closer

Today, I speak to you in hope that you will come closer. Draw near to Me. I love you unconditionally. I have what belongs to you. I want to satisfy you through and through.

Please slow down some. Don't be in a hurry. Why do you stay so busy? It is in the quiet moments that I heal. Your full purpose is found when you are quiet and still.

There is time for everything in the earth, and now is your time to draw close. Draw close so I can speak to you. Draw close so I can show you things concerning your life. Draw close so I can heal you. Draw close so I can love on you. Draw close so you will be strengthened. Draw close so you will deepen your relationship with me. It will enable you to know me more.

This is a 911. I call this a state of emergency. It is imperative that you seek me in sincerity. Times are changing quickly. I'm drawing you in secret. Don't you feel the wooing, the nudging, the tugging deep within your soul? I want to reveal to you so much, that you may share much with others.

I am your refuge. I am your safety. I am your protector. I am your rear guard. I am your provider. I am your strong tower. I am the one who wants to revive you. This is a 911. There is no better time than now.

Mouth to mouth ... draw closer.

Prayer

Father, today I want to thank You for the drawing. I confess that it is a state of an emergency, and I ask Your forgiveness for not drawing close to You. I run to You today expecting You to reveal secrets of the kingdom, in Jesus' Name, Amen.

Prophetic Declaration

I declare today is a 911 to draw close. I declare secrets are being revealed now. I decree it! It is so NOW, and so shall it be!

Notes

_____

_____

_____

_____

_____

_____

_____

_____

_____

_____

_____

_____

Day 10

Many are the plans in the mind of a man, but it is the purpose of the Lord that will stand.
Proverbs 19:21
English Standard Version

control:
to exercise restraint or direction over; dominate; command.

I Want Total Control

If you let Me be in control it will turn out fine. I am redeeming you by the power of My great hand. It all begins at this moment right now. I am removing old patterns. I am requiring you to do away with old behaviors. I am requiring you to put away old ways all because I want you to be totally free.

Allow My Word to consume you. I work all things out pertaining to your life according to the counsel of My will. I formed the light just as I created the darkness. I made all things for Myself. So, with that being said, just know that I made you.

The fight that you have been in is because of your refusal to allow Me to be in total control of your life. Give up the need to know. Give up the need to direct. Give up your need to correct, and please give up your need to dictate to Me. Take pleasure in knowing that I, the Lord, know what is best for you. It gives Me joy to lead every detail of your life.

You are so used to your habitual ways and daily patterns that it keeps you from absolute freedom. Gently surrender to My will for your life. Trust me today, knowing that all things are going to work out for your good as you allow Me to be in control. My plans and purpose will stand. Give Me permission to have total control.

Mouth to mouth ... I want total control.

Prayer

Father, today I ask You to help me with my control issues. I ask that You work out every detail of my life as I willingly yield to You, in Jesus' Name, Amen.

Prophetic Declaration

I declare today that God is in total control of my life, and His plan will prevail and stand. I have spoken it! I decree it! It is so, Now!

Notes

Day 11

He changes times and seasons; he deposes kings and raises up others. He gives wisdom to the wise and knowledge to the discerning.
Daniel 2:21
New International Version

time:
plan, schedule, or arrange when (something) should happen or be done

This Is The Time

This is the time. I have so much in store for you. Do not buy and settle for the lies of the enemy. Renew your mind daily. The mind is where the attacks are. Satan is the enemy of your soul.

You must learn to rest in My presence. It is there that you find life. It is there that you get renewed strength. It is there that you find purpose. It is there you find the courage to proceed forward.

This is the time for you to seek Me with all of your heart. As you seek Me, I will release the divine strategies necessary to fulfill every directive I've already given you. What you need for this time is found in My presence. Did I not say that in My presence is fullness of joy? It is in our time together that all your fears fade away. I have made a way of escape for you today. This is the time now to release all that you have allowed to hold you captive. This is your time to sing, and in your barrenness you will produce.

You have what it takes to move forward. Go! I am with you. You and your household will be fine. I want to unveil to you the riches of My Glory, the treasures of My Glory, the abundance released in My Glory! It is hidden for you, dear one, and available now.

You have settled long enough. I want to give you everything that I have promised. Yes, you can have it ALL. I speak to you today that your time is now, and yes, this is My set time to endow you with favor. This is your appointed time!

Mouth to mouth ... this is the time.

Prayer

Father, I thank You today for giving me strength. I ask You to release the captivity of my mind to renewed purpose. Give me an awareness of Your constant nearness to me that I may lay hold to the riches of Your glory, in Jesus' Name, Amen.

Prophetic Declaration

I declare that this is the time for me to receive renewed visions and receive a greater release of your Glory upon me. I have spoken it! I decree it! It is so, NOW!

Notes

Day 12

*May He grant your heart's desires and make all your plans
succeed. May we shout for joy when we hear of your victory and raise
a victory banner in the name of our God.
May the Lord answer all your prayers.*
Psalm 20:4-5
The Living Translation

happen:
to come into being or occur as an event, process, or result

It Will Happen

I am going to bless My children. This is a time when I am making My promises good. I know it may seem as if I have forgotten, but you must be strong in faith and stand on My Word, knowing, believing, and trusting that I am well able to deliver.

Remember that this is your time and season for great victory. I, the Lord, will give you your heart's desires. All you need to do is ask Me. It gives Me pleasure to do good to My children. Don't be afraid to dream big. Refuse to continue living in fear from past regrets, from disappointments, and especially from living according to the opinions of others. This is the day I am granting all your heart can dream and desire; but it must be in alignment with My will for your life. This is the day that I cause your plans to succeed. Only, ask to make My desires become your desires, and watch them quickly come to pass.

Come on, My child, it's time to dream again. It's your moment to live again! It's your season to laugh, dance, and love again! I've given you only one life to live. Today, make a decision to live your best life now. Embrace this day with courage and hope, knowing that if I be for you, then who can ever stop your plans from succeeding.

Get up from the place of mourning and complaining. You've got no time for self pity. It's time to forget past failures. Launch out into the deep! It is time. Tell yourself, "This day I am rising above my mess and moving into my message." What is your message? It is speaking loudly. Listen! It is your destiny! Your destiny is the message! Your life speaks to others when you think no one is listening at all.

Don't allow anything or anyone to stop you anymore – not even yourself. I am rooting for you, and I declare this day I am backing up your success. I call all of heaven and My Word as a witness. Shout for joy now knowing that I will answer all your requests. Ask Me today; I am waiting.

Mouth to mouth ... it will happen.

Prayer

Father, I thank you today that I am released from my past regrets and failures. I will no longer look at what could have been or should have been. I ask for your power to live in my moment right now. I release and forgive so that I can move forward and succeed, in Jesus' Name, Amen.

Prophetic Declaration

I declare today that IT WILL HAPPEN. I speak to my dreams and desires and say, "Live!" I have spoken it! I decree it! It is so, NOW!

Notes

Day 13

*May He equip you with all you need for doing His will. May He
produce in you, through the power of Jesus Christ, every good thing
that is pleasing to Him. All glory to Him forever and ever! Amen.*

Hebrews 13:21
New Living Translation

Equipped:

supplied with the necessary items for a particular purpose; prepared
(someone) mentally for a particular situation or task

Equipped To Serve

Today child, just know that you are equipped with all that you
need. I have endowed you with spiritual tools. Before the
foundations of time, I put in you all that you would require to assist
you in fulfilling your destiny. I have bestowed upon you the gifts of
My Spirit. I have provided you access through faith. I have made
available to you manifold wisdom. I have granted you
understanding. I have showered you with the fruits of My Spirit. I
have imparted the anointing to remove burdens and destroy yokes. I
have given you ALL— all you need to walk in the assignment that was
prearranged for a particular point in time— way before you were
knit together in your mother's womb.

All you must do is agree with Me and put your trust in Me. I am
the Ancient of days. This is the portion from Me that is a gift and
your inheritance.

You have been equipped to do Kingdom business. You should feel
your sense of entitlement rising up even at this moment. Your
birthright–destiny–heritage equips you for every God given
assignment you must carry out on this earth. Life has prepared you

for this time. You are spiritually, mentally, and physically groomed for this moment in your life.

Mouth to mouth ... you are equipped to serve.

Prayer

Father, I thank You today for equipping me with everything I need to move forward. I ask You to give me wisdom for Kingdom business, in Jesus' Name, Amen.

Prophetic Declaration

I declare today that I am equipped to serve in every capacity in the Kingdom of God. I have spoken it! I decree it! It is so, NOW!

Notes

Day 14

Now set your heart and your soul to seek the Lord your God; arise, therefore, and build the sanctuary of the Lord God, so that you may bring the ark of the covenant of the Lord and the holy vessels of God into the house that is to be built for the name of the Lord.

1 Chronicles 22:19
New King James Version

Pursue:

to find or employ measures to obtain or accomplish: seek <pursue a goal>

Pursue It Regardless

I know it seems that all odds are stacked against you right now. But the truth is it's all a twisted lie. Cast down for what? Shrink back for what? No way! I dare not hear of it! Do you realize the price that was paid? Get a revelation of what's been done!

Imagination is My gift to you. You don't have to have every detail mapped out; you only need to move forward and obey. Every step you take must be according to that which My spirit speaks silently in your ear. Away with the lies that you have believed! It's time to step out in the supernatural and do it anyway. My Kingdom is available to you NOW!

Open your heart and enter in. It is simple; just be as a little child. My Kingdom is accessible, reachable, and available at all times. Move forward and pursue the greater regardless of your current situation, regardless of what people may say, and regardless of what lies the enemy may have persuaded you to believe.

As I once told My servant, David, it is time to pursue, overtake, and recover all. I am the same God today as I was to my servant, then. Position yourself to seek me for divine strategy. I have given you all the anointing you need. Rise up today and pursue it regardless − and just in case you are wondering what IT is−it is the INTENDED THING that I have ordained, created, and purposed for you in this moment in time.

Mouth to mouth ... pursue it regardless.

Prayer

Father, I ask You today to give me the courage to withstand the forces of the enemy that would persuade me to walk away from the intended thing that You have purposed for my life in this season, in Jesus' Name, Amen.

Prophetic Declaration

I declare I am pursuing my destiny, regardless. I have spoken it! I decree it! It is so, NOW!

Notes

Day 15

For You, Lord, will bless the [uncompromisingly] righteous [him who is upright and in right standing with You]; as with a shield You will surround him with goodwill (pleasure and favor).

Psalm 5:12

Amplified Bible

Right:

restore to a normal or upright position.

It's Right

I have worked out all things for the righteous. Are you not My right one? It's not because of what you do, but it's simply because of who and whose you are. Nothing can stop you, for I will be before you, after you, and all around you. Nothing can separate you from My love. It's My love that will carry you through this next season.

Today I want you to embrace your future with hope and earnest expectation. The earth is waiting in travail for you to shine forth. Truly, I say to you that your best years are here— right now. The time for your desires to be fulfilled is now.

Nothing happens without a price. You have paid it in prayer, in fasting and, lest I forget, in sufferings. I have chosen you this day; you have not chosen Me. I have called you; you didn't call me. Set your face like a flint and cry out from your position of being My righteous vessel.

Your times are in My hands, and so are you. Nothing or no one can harm you or take you out of My divine purpose. Only you can stagnate My promises. I will perform My good word toward you. No one has the power to dictate what I originate. No one can alter My will for your life. What I do is always right.

Mouth to mouth ... it's right!

Prayer

Father, I ask You today to remind me by the Holy Spirit of the price You paid for me to be declared your right one. I thank You from making me right and altering all that was ever wrong, in Jesus' Name, Amen.

Prophetic Declaration

I declare today that God will perform His good word toward me. I declare I am the righteousness of God. I have spoken it! I decree it! It is so, NOW!

Notes

Day 16

His divine power has granted to us all things that pertain to life and godliness, through the knowledge of Him who called us to his own glory and excellence
2 Peter 1:3
English Standard Version

All:

the whole of one's possessions, energy, or interest.

It's All Up to You!!

I have given you everything you need pertaining to life and godliness. You have My permission to exercise My authority in every given situation you face on this earth. You are mine, and nothing or no one can ever change that. All that you are comes from Me and through Me. That is why I say it is all up to you. It is all up to you to walk in what I have declared to you!! Access is granted to those who will only believe.

A greater glory is still yet to be seen. A greater story is still yet to be told. I am with you. Yes, I am for you, and I have even gone before you to make every crooked road straight, every high place low, and every rough place smooth. Victory or defeat is all up to you.

You can choose to move to the top or stay living on the bottom. When I say live on top, I mean in revelation, insight, miracles, signs, wonders; and literally, expelling every lie of the enemy. Living on the bottom means you live as a victim. You live as though I have not done anything at all to change your current condition or your current situation.

Remember what I said; you have access to all things in the heavens that gives you access in the earth. I have called you to a greater glory that will change the outcome of your story!!! It's all up to you whether or not you stay here or decide to rise up and break through. I have given you the power. You decide.

Mouth to mouth ... it's all up to you.

Prayer

Father, today I won't ask for anything. But I lift my hands and say, "Thank You," for all that You have given me pertaining to life and godliness. Thank You for access and victory as I take charge of my life and walk into all that you have given to me this day, in Jesus' Name, Amen.

Prophetic Declaration

I declare victory in every area of my life as I rise, decreeing I have been given all things pertaining to life and godliness. I have spoken it! I decree it! It is so, NOW!

Notes

Day 17

I will instruct thee and teach thee the way in which thou shalt go; I will counsel [thee]
with mine eye upon thee.
Psalm 32:8
Darby Bible Translation

Lead:

to go before or with; to show the way; conduct or escort: to guide in direction, course, action, opinion, etc.;

Surely I Will Lead You

I will lead you in a way that you have not known or heard. I will lead you by My Spirit. Let My word be your guide.

This day I have opened a wide door for you. It is a door of opportunity. It is a door of plenty. It is a door of blessings. It is a door of ministry. It is a door of favor. It is a door of great reward. It is a door of breakthrough. It is a door of deliverance. It is a door of promise. This door will connect you to all that I have told you of before.

Only do not fear; just walk through the door. The door speaks of divine connections, divine hook-ups, and even divine set ups. The doors resemble the gateway to glory. Rise up in faith and walk through the door. Even as I told my servant Paul—with an opportunity as great as this comes many adversaries.

But My child, there is no need to worry; I have already won the battle for you. As a matter of fact, there is no need for you to fight in this one. I will take care of everything. You just need to stay in faith, and the victory will be handed over to you as promised.

I assure you this day that I am leading you by My righteous hand and guiding you with My eye. This is a certifiable release of the rains being poured out in your life—the moment when you can say, "Truly, 'my latter is greater than my former' has now arrived." It is what we agreed to even before the beginning of time.

Embrace all that is yours. Only, let My Spirit be your tour guide as you journey in this life. I am waiting to lead you.

Mouth to mouth ... and surely, I will lead you.

Prayer

Father, today I ask that You lead me by Your Spirit as I, in faith, walk through the open door. Help me not to look back or hold on to anything that You are disconnecting me from in this season, in Jesus' Name, Amen.

Prophetic Declaration

I declare today the Holy Spirit is leading me in the way that I need to go. I have spoken it! I decree it! It is so, NOW!

Notes

Day 18

Only let each person lead the life that the Lord has assigned to him, and to which God has called him ...
1 Corinthians 7:17
English Standard Version

assignment:
a task or piece of work assigned to someone as part of a job or course of study.

Pushed Into Your Assignment

There are people and things that are assigned to you that I have ordained; there are people and things assigned to you that you have personally ordained; and moreover, there are people and things assigned to you that the enemy has ordained. Therefore, My mission for your life must be clear.

The assignment that I have given to YOU must take priority over everything else. It is so easy to become distracted because there are so many voices in the earth. You have a voice; your friends and family have a voice; your past has a voice; and even the enemy comes to you with his voice. In order to stay the course, I have laid out for you, you must obey My voice. My voice will align you for destiny. My voice assures you that you are in purpose. My voice dictates the course of direction as well as correction.

Do not be manipulated out of your assignment. Refuse to be talked out of your assignment. There are so many things you can do, but one that I have chosen you to do. The assignment that I have given to you is crucial. It is connected to so much more than you. Get you out of the way, sit at My feet, and allow Me to give you the strategy to be pushed into your assignment.

How do I know my assignment, you may be asking? It is the thing that you dream about. It is the thing you never get tired of doing. It is the thing you were put here on this earth to do. It is the thing that drives you even when you have no desire to be driven. It is your assignment that I am pushing you into right now.

Your education can't put you there. Your wisdom won't get you there. Your intellectual knowledge means nothing in that place called "there." Who you know has nothing to do with getting you there. It's who you are, My child, that the price has been paid for you to sit there. Your assignment is to know who you are and rise up in this revelation and insight that pushes you into your assignment in this earth.

Let Me push you today. It all starts with simply knowing who you are. You are assigned to Me as I have been assigned to you, and that pushes you into the assignment that I have ordained for your life. You, My child, have been assigned to do great things. Yes, even miracles, signs, and wonders will follow you when you are in your assignment. I am pushing you because it's time to take hold of your divine assignment.

Mouth to mouth ... you've been pushed into your assignment.

Prayer

Father, I ask today that You will help me to step out into my divine assignment by removing every obstacle that wants to stand in my way. I ask You to remove any voice that is contrary to Your will for my life, in Jesus' Name, Amen.

Prophetic Declaration

I declare that I am walking in my divine assignment, and nothing or no one can stop me. I have spoken it! I decree it! It is so, NOW!

Notes

Day 19

"Then I will set the key of the house of David on his shoulder, When he opens no one will shut, When he shuts no one will open.
Isaiah 22:22
New American Standard Bible

Door:
a movable structure used for opening and closing an entrance or for giving access to something.

Open Doors That NO MAN Can CLOSE!!!!

I have given you access. What are you waiting for? Who are you waiting on? All things are through Me and all things are for Me. Nothing can get past Me. The enemy is waiting for your fall, for your fail to no prevail. But here is the good news: you will not fall; and you cannot fail; and he definitely will not prevail.

I have opened the doors for you. Only be careful to acknowledge what I am doing and have done, and especially what I am going to do in you, through you, for you, and most definitely around you. I am the only faithful God. I am that I am, and I am the I am of the Lord— the open door. Who can dare shut what I have opened? You must take advantage of every moment that I have given when the opportunity is presented to you.

Today I have Opened Doors all around you. They are doors of peace, joy, love, prosperity, ministry opportunity, and many, many more. But mainly the doors I have opened are doors of your heart which represent your past, present, and future. I am also shutting the doors of your past that would love to paralyze you and hold you hostage.

Well, today I am declaring you are no longer a prisoner of your past. The war is over, and the door is opened to walk free. I, the Lord of past, present, and future say I have shut the door, and you are free to walk into your glorious moment called NOW. I am the door. Now who shall contend with that? Again, who dare CLOSE what I have opened? The door is opened, so openly walk through it. Keeping this in mind, remember that I am the God of all Doors and, to you, I have granted access.

Mouth to mouth ... the doors are opened and no man can close.

Prayer

Father, help me to be reminded today that Jesus is the door. Forgive me for expecting people to do for me that which only comes through You. I accept Your plan for every opened and closed door in my life, in Jesus' Name, Amen.

Prophetic Declaration

I declare today that every door of success and opportunity ordained by God is available to me now. I have spoken it! I decree it! It is so, NOW!

Notes

Day 20

So we must make every effort to enter that place of rest ...
Hebrews 4:11a
GOD'S Word Translation

Rest:
freedom from activity or labor

Labor To Rest

You are way too busy for ME. All your meetings and engagements must stop. You have no time for Me, much less time for yourself. When will enough really be enough! Between social media, your social life and your trying to keep up with the status quo, you have forgotten that I am He from which your life source flows. Labor to rest in My presence; then you will find joy, hope, peace and faith to continue your journey. Know that I have a desired destination for you.

The warfare on the journey is real. The enemy desires to sift your soul. But I have intervened again. You must slow down. Let your "YES" BE TO ME ONLY and your "NO" to the demands and commands of projects, people, and being an ultimate men pleaser. The seasons have changed. Discern where you are in terms of kingdom dynamics.

The war is already won. That is the revelation the enemy of your soul doesn't want you to comprehend. I sent My son to die for everything. Now, contend for WHAT? I settled every issue. I paid the price with BLOOD because it was the required sacrifice. Your sweat and tears will never be enough to satisfy the price. Quit allowing the devil to have you bring offerings of your flesh.

This is what you need to do ... 1) Quit wrestling! You will never win this one with your flesh. (Ephesians 6:12); 2) Get a revelation of what I have done for you and a clear understanding of who you are!! (Colossians 2:15); 3) Pray for wisdom and enlightenment to understand the seasons and times concerning My will for your life!! (Daniel 2:21); 4) Seek me with everything as if your life depends on it. (Psalm 105:4)

Love me regardless. Let nothing separate us. Remember the price has been paid and the way has already been made. Take time and make time to rest. It is imperative in this season. Your labor is only to find rest as My servant.

Mouth to mouth ... labor to rest.

Prayer

Father, I thank You for reminding me of my constant busyness. Forgive me for allowing people and social engagements to dictate my destiny. I accept Your rest, in Jesus' name, Amen.

Prophetic Declaration

I declare I am in sync with God's season for my life because I labor to rest. I decree it! I declare it is so, and so shall it be, NOW!

Notes

Day 21

For it was I, the Lord your God, who rescued you from the land of Egypt. Open your mouth wide, and I will fill it with good things.
Psalm 81:10
New Living Translation

Open:

allowing access, passage, or a view through an empty space; not closed or blocked up.

Open Your Mouth

This is a year of prophetic fulfillment. You will see every word that I have spoken begin to manifest before your eyes as you seek Me with your whole heart. I will open your eyes and your understanding to reveal and unveil the plan the enemy has devised to frustrate you, to deter you, to silence you, and to bring you to a place of desolation and spiritual ruin.

I am commanding you to OPEN YOUR MOUTH WIDE, open your mouth and I WILL fill it. As you raise your voice like a trumpet, your voice will speak to the desolations in the land, and fertile ground will appear. Your voice will send demons to flight. Your voice will cause blind eyes to open, and deaf ears will come unstopped. Your voice will be what I use for My Glory to be made manifest in the earth.

Set your face like a flint. Don't look to the right or the left. I want to use you in a way that you have never been used before. Empty yourselves and come with a spirit of humility; and then you will see what has been prophesied through My Prophets of old.

That Glory will rise on you in darkness. Yes, gross darkness is covering the earth, but you, My Prophets, are the ones that I am pouring My glory upon because of the enemy's tactics to destroy My people.

You were not created to be a voice of "REASON", but a voice in "SEASON." This is your season called "NOW." Activate what is on the inside of you. It is time to SPEAK LIFE, DECLARE LIFE, SHOUT LIFE. Prophesy not what you feel; but Prophesy what I am saying, and not one word will fall to the ground, because there is always a performance when I SPEAK. NO LONGER WILL THERE BE A LINGERING EFFECT; FOR THE MOMENT YOU SPEAK, WATCH FOR THE MANIFESTION. IT'S HAPPENING NOW, NOW, NOW! RISE UP MAN, RISE UP WOMEN AND DECLARE RIGHT NOW!

Mouth to mouth ... it's time to open your mouth!

Prayer

Father, I thank You today that as I open my mouth, You will fill it. I ask You to fill my mouth with good things. I submit myself to Your word and will speak only those words that will give life, in Jesus' Name, Amen.

Prophetic Declaration

I declare today that the words I speak in faith will not fall to the ground. I say what God has commanded me to say and I see miraculous results. I have spoken it! I decree it! It is so, NOW!

Notes

Day 22

But I have something against you, because you have left your former love.
Revelation 2:4
Aramaic Bible in Plain English

Passion:
a love affair

Where Is Your Passion?

It's time to Romance the King. You have lost your first love. Come back to Me. You were created for Me. You were created to give Me love. But most of all, you were created for the secret place. It is in that place that you are healed. It is in that place that you are filled. It is in that place that you get peace. It is in that place I give renewed purpose. It is in that place you receive strength for your journey.

You are mine until the end. I want you to make a commitment to me today. Let's renew our vows. Decide today that you choose Me in the best and even the worst. I remind you that I made an everlasting covenant with you. I want you blessed. I want you whole. I want you to be Mine. Together we are writing a story that will touch the world. When others see the results of our love affair they should be motivated and inspired to want the same.

Oh, how I want you to come back to Me! I really miss you. I am not angry. I have been waiting for a long time. Come to Me and I will make you passionate for Me again.

Mouth to mouth ... where is your passion?

Prayer

Father, I come to You today repenting for leaving You, my first love. I am asking You, today, to draw me to You. I am ready to put You in first place again. This is my earnest request, in Jesus' Name, Amen.

Prophetic Declaration

I declare today that my romance with God, Jesus and Holy Spirit is being rekindled, reignited, and refueled. I have spoken it! I decree it! It is so, NOW!!

Notes

Day 23

Faith assures us of things we expect and convinces us of the existence of things we cannot see.
Hebrews 11:1
GOD'S WORD® Translation

Faith:

complete confidence or trust in a person or thing; or a belief not based on proof.

Release Your Faith

Nothing happens in the kingdom unless you release it by faith. You know what faith is. It is My word on your situation, released at the right moment, that shifts the outcome of your life and your surroundings forever. Today I want you to release your faith for miracles. Release your faith for healing. Replace your fear with faith, My dear. Indulge in My word.

Faith is the final say so in all matters. When you release your faith, dead things come to life. Old things are restored. Failure is replaced with success. Faith released brings favor in your life. Hopelessness is changed to hope. Faith is the way I operate in the earth. Without it you can't please Me; and of course, you know faith without works is dead. You have within you faith that can move mountains. I want you to release your faith for the lost and for the backslider. Release your faith for your miracle. I am the God that requires FAITH. Faith is the assurance that I can do what I said. Faith is the secret to manifesting My Goodness in the earth. You are no different than the generals of faith who have gone before you. Faith is trusting every word I have ever spoken and clinging to it as if it was the only survival mechanism left in the earth.

Release your faith, I say! Release your faith and watch Me move on your behalf. My word spoken on your situation releases My anointing into your situation which produces transformation, freedom, and deliverance every time.

Mouth to mouth ... it is time to release your faith.

Prayer

Father, today, by the unction of Holy Spirit, help me to be mindful to speak faith filled words in every situation of my life, in Jesus' Name, Amen.

Prophetic Declaration

I declare I am a faith releasing kingdom machine operating in the same faith of Jesus. I have said it! I believe it; and NOW it is so, and so shall it be!

Notes

Day 24

But the Lord said to Samuel, "Do not look on his appearance or on the height of his stature, because I have rejected him. For the Lord sees not as man sees: man looks on the outward appearance, but the Lord looks on the heart.
1 Samuel 16:7
English Standard Version

Expression:

the process of making known one's thoughts or feelings

My Prophetic Expression

You will speak My words of Truth, for you are My prophetic expression in the earth. You are My voice that will prophecy to nations. You must have clear insight and know exactly what I am doing. Do not be afraid of the expressions of terror in the earth. They will last only for a moment.

Suddenly, I will intervene on your behalf. You have nothing to lose, only much to be gained. The time of your departure is very soon. You are leaving your old place of sickness, lack, doubt, hopelessness and negativity now. Only be diligent to obey all that I say. Don't fight the process. For there is a work to be done in the earth, and I choose to do it through you.

You are made in MY prophetic image. I am activating your prophetic voice and stirring up your prophetic creativity. Doors are opening that will give you awesome opportunities for prophetic advancement. Only be steadfast, and I will lead you step by step. There is an unfolding and unveiling of secret things; but you must listen attentively for My voice in the quiet of the night. It is there. I will show you things to come.

Oh, I have so much in store for you. Launch out into the deep. It is calling you. Dive into the treasures that have been stored away for you —dreams, prophetic visions, and revelation. Don't rely on any wisdom of your own. Rely only on Me. When I say your own wisdom, I mean your intellect, your flesh, your dependence on others – that which you are most familiar with; those things that would keep you in your comfort zone.

Step out. Step in. Step up into the next realm of glory. It is time to leave from this place of glory to go to your next place. I call that the realm of faith and the realm of glory which is necessary to function prophetically. This is the next season of glory, titled your prophetic moment. I am uttering to you like the voice that speaks on the waters. It is easy. All you must do is stand up and move forward. Nations are waiting on YOU. It's My choosing, not yours.

Mouth to mouth ... you are my prophetic expression.

Prayer

Father help me to transition with grace. I am aware that You are moving me from one dimension to the next. I believe; but today, I need You to help my unbelief. I am ready to move forward so I will not miss what you have in store for my life. Thank You in advance for making this a smooth transition, in Jesus' Name, Amen.

Prophetic Declaration

I decree that I am in sync with God's will for the prophetic call on my life. My life is God's prophetic interpretation in the earth. I believe it! I declare it! It is so, NOW!

Notes

Day 25

And teach me to do your pleasure, because you are my God; your
Spirit is sweet; you will lead me in the way of life.
Psalm 143:10
Aramaic Bible in Plain English

Let:

not prevent or forbid; allow.

Let Me Do It

What you have seen Me do ... now I say to you ... do the same. I have given you wisdom, instructions, and power to fulfill My will in the earth. Let Me say ... this is a time where you must draw close for your next assignment. It is a season where you are mandated to draw so near to Me you will be able to hear My heartbeat. If you are familiar with what I love most, you will understand that My heart beats for the "SOUL of a MAN."

The days of your watching from the sidelines are over. The days of spectating, hesitating, and anticipating are done. The days of observing the game and not playing the game are finished. You are not a substitute. You are not a fill-in. It is time to get in the game of life. You are a starter– one who will start fires. You are one called who will birth an outpouring that no one will be able to claim, name, or maintain. You are one chosen who will spark the turning of the upcoming generations to Me!!!

I said it!!! This is not an instruction to the buildings and empires that you have so perfectly designed; but this is to My Kingdom, which is not a physical place as you suppose. The kingdom has always been designed for My rule in the hearts of all of mankind willfully submitted to Me in love.

How can I do this, you may be asking? You can't. Let Me do it through you by your obedience to the leading of Holy Spirit. He will instruct you, guide you, and whisper to you step by step. You have been appointed, anointed, and endowed with power. Yield to Me, and I will lead the way. Only Let Me do It, and you will experience the miraculous.

Mouth to mouth ... let me do it.

Prayer

Father, today I am asking You that You will be my guide. I allow You to work through me. I allow You to spark a flame so big in me that I will give light to others along my way. I thank You for a supernatural drawing that will bring me closer to You. I want to hear Your heartbeat, and I am asking You to make me a fisher for the souls of men, in Jesus' Name, Amen.

Prophetic Declaration

I decree that I am a fire starter and a birther of the supernatural power of the Almighty GOD. I declare it and believe that it is so NOW, and so shall it be!

Notes

Day 26

For I know the thoughts that I think concerning you, said the Lord, thoughts of peace, and not of evil, to give you the end that you wait for.
Jeremiah 29:11
Jubilee Bible 2000

Role:

the function assumed or part played by a person or thing in a particular situation.

What Is Your Role?

You are a spokesman for Me. You were created for My pleasure. You do not have to audition to be yourself. You were created to admonish. You were created to direct. You were created to influence. You were created to win. You were created to be the head and never, ever the tail. You were created to shift nations. You were created as an intercessor. You were created with purpose in mind. You were never just a thought to Me. You were always MY LIVING REALITY!!!

Are you getting it now? You are the apple of My eye. To Me, you are just perfect. You are My partner in the earth. You were created for miracles. You were created to worship Me. You were created for My GOOD pleasure. You were created with the end in mind. You were created for greatness. You were created to bring Me joy. You are My masterpiece. You are My jewel. You are My royalty. You are created in My image.

Is that not enough? Oh, but I can go on. You were designed to overcome every obstacle. You were shaped and fashioned by the works of My hand. Before you were in your mother's womb, I knew

YOU. I loved YOU! I equipped YOU!! I knew everything that you would do. You cannot surprise Me.

What is YOUR Role? Your role is to love Me with all your heart, mind, soul, body and strength. Your role is to love your neighbor as yourself. Your role is to simply obey me. That is your role! You need no permission, nor a script to fulfill your role.

Mouth to mouth ... remember your role.

Prayer

Father help me today to be the you that You have created me to be. I repent for role playing and diminishing myself in the presence of others around whom I may not be comfortable being my true self. I receive your word that you know why you created me. Thank you for helping me adjust every secret thought of not being good enough, in Jesus' Name, Amen.

Prophetic Declaration

I declare today that I am the best Me that My God has created me to be. I am a powerful me. I am a wise me. I am a glorious me; and I declare I am true to me. I decree it and it is so NOW, and so shall it be!

Notes

Day 27

...wist ye not that I must be about my Father's business?
Luke 2:49b
King James Version

Business:
organization or economic system where goods and services are exchanged for one another

Finished Business

I know things may seem a little out of sorts; but I need you to know that at this point in your life I am dealing with all the scattered pieces in your life. I am the God who knows how to handle business.

I settled everything with My blood. Who told you that My blood was not enough? It paid the price. It covered your sins. My blood justified you. It purchased you. It overthrew the powers of darkness. My blood redeemed you. It drew you near, gave you peace, cleared your conscious, washed you clean and sanctified you. The cross was an outward expression of finished business. Let it be enough.

When the enemy comes in remind him that you are an overcomer by My blood and the word of your testimony. I feel I need to remind you once more that MY BLOOD resolved ... and now opens doors. It delivered you, healed you, established you, and made you whole. Through My blood you have been granted access and set up for abundance, prosperity, and promised success. The life of the flesh is in the blood. Now can there be any greater victory than that? My blood still speaks.

Finished business ... I remind you today the debt has been paid and the foundation laid. The only thing there is for you to do is finish what I started and get busy about your Father's business. Greater works shall you do because you believe. It's time to transact Kingdom business in the spirit realm. Let's get it done!

Mouth to mouth ... it is finished!

Prayer

Father, I want to thank You today for taking my place and transacting business with Your blood on my behalf. I ask for clearer insight into all that Your blood has provided for me, in Jesus' Name, Amen.

Prophetic Declaration

I decree that the blood of Jesus activates every promise in my life today. I declare it! I believe it is so NOW, and so shall it be!

Notes

Day 28

And if a man says anything to you, say to him, 'They are needed by our Lord', and immediately he will send them here.
Matthew 21:3
Aramaic Bible in Plain English

Need:

require (something) because it is essential or very important.

I Have A Need

With things in your world as chaotic as they are, I am pleading to you, for I have a need. It is essential to you to not be hasty but realize that I am spewing things up in the earth. The earth is groaning for the birthing and manifestation of my sons and daughters coming forth, because I have a need.

You are probably wondering ... how could a God so great need me? I'll tell you why I need you. I need you to be who I created you to be. I need you to demonstrate My anointing in the earth. I need you to daily put on your armor; and don't be caught off guard by the attacks of the enemy. I need you to study to show yourself approved. I need you to guard your heart with all diligence. I need you to think on heavenly things. I need you to be aware that you are not wrestling against flesh and blood, but against a kingdom of darkness that is strongly trying to influence and persuade you to be divided. I need you to lay hands on the sick. I need you to cast out demons. I need you to give Me room in your daily schedules. I need you to praise Me. I need you to worship Me. I need you to esteem Me higher than anything in your life.

I NEED YOU!!! I need you to trust Me. I need you to believe Me. I need you to live by My words alone. I need you to pray. I need you to fast. I need you to be My witness in the earth. I need you to be bold. I need you to be courageous. I need you to stand in the face of adversity using My word to demolish strongholds. I need you to open your mouth and speak. I need you to not be afraid.

I am relying on you because I know what I want from you. I need you to win souls; and in doing so, you are considered to be wise. I need you to allow Me to INTERPRET what your NOW is supposed to look like. I need you to stop working in your flesh and start moving by My spirit. I need you to let your failures, your past, and your disappointments go. I need you to only allow Me to settle and establish you. I need you to lean on Me for everything. I need you to do this for Me.

Lastly, I need you to only be the you that I have created you to be. One more thing ... I need My church ... My body ... My called out ones to unite together as One. I need you to be still and know that I am God. I need My Bride to ARISE. SEE? ... I do have needs.

Mouth to mouth ... I have a need.

Prayer

Father, today I ask You to put me in the place where You need me the most. Help me to arise to the occasion to be the answer and solution to the world's problem. Remind me today that all of mankind is in dire need of a Savior. I accept the responsibility of being light in darkness. Again, thank you, in Jesus' Name, Amen.

Prophetic Declaration

I decree and declare that what God needs today is active and flowing through me. I decree it! It is so NOW, and so shall it be!

Notes

Day 29

The Lord will accomplish what concerns me; Your lovingkindness, O Lord, is everlasting; Do not forsake the works of Your hands.

Psalm 138:8
New American Standard Bible

Want:

have a desire to possess or do (something); wish for

You Have to Want IT!

I created you with purpose in mind. Yes, I do have a plan for your life—one greater than you could ever imagine. So, stay true to the vision I have laid before you.

The enemy will use all he can to disrupt you, distract you, and take you off course. But I will lead you by My spirit every step of the way. Only wait in times of prayer and worship to hear the still small voice that will usher you into purpose. I have an ordained path cleared out for you. My word will be, for you, a lamp to Your feet, and will definitely lighten your path.

Let not the unknown make you settle for less. You must want it. You must be driven with passion to walk in your purpose. Yes, war is waged against you; but remember, the battle has been won. Begin to get a desire for more. Don't succumb to the voices, though at times there are so many. You know when I speak, and it is the sounding board that leads the way to destiny.

How bad do you want it? ... the goals you have been desiring; the dreams you have talked about; and the vision you have glimpsed. Do you want it bad enough to pursue it? Get back to the place of total surrender. I know you may not know what to do to cause your deepest desires to come to pass, but I do. Press into Me with your thanksgiving and praise and trust the architect of your life with the blueprints. Trust Me. I know what I am doing. I just need you to start dreaming again.

Will you begin believing again? Won't you allow Me to lead the way? Please get a passion for purpose on the inside of you. Desire, devotion, dedication and diligence is all that is required. How bad do you want it? Take up your bed. Let's move away from this place. It's time to walk into IT! No one can cancel your destiny but you. No one can stop it but YOU!! You have all the necessary ingredients. Go for IT!!! My word has creative potential. Declare IT! Speak IT! Decree IT! Pray IT! Stand on IT! Sing IT! Watch miracles take place!

Mouth to Mouth ... How bad do you want it?

Prayer

Father, I ask You to unfold Your master plan for my life. I am submitted to You as the architect of every design and layout specifically sketched by Your hands for me. Let Your grace overtake me as I yield to my IT (purpose), in Jesus' Name, Amen.

Prophetic Declaration

I declare that my "want" to walk in my destiny is arising in me greater than ever before. Nothing can stop me, for I have been born for purpose that produces miracles. I decree it and declare it! It is so NOW, and so shall it be.

Notes

Day 30

Absolutely not! Let God be proven true, and every human being shown up as a liar, just as it is written...
Romans 3:4
NET Bible

Argue:

exchange or express diverging or opposite views, typically in a heated or angry way.

Don't Argue with Me!

You didn't choose Me; I chose you. I formed you in your mother's womb. I know how you operate. Please don't disagree with Me. Stop questioning your existence. I selected the weak things to confound the wise. I know what you have been through ... so many challenges and so much adversity in your life span. Please don't adapt and conform yourself to your conditions and the opinions of others. When you make these negative arguments within yourself you come against the authentic you I created you to be; and everything about you becomes a lie.

How dare you argue with My creative design! How dare you not agree with Me! How dare you believe the lies of the enemy! Please don't continue to argue with the truth. The truth is, in Me, you are a conqueror ... the head, first, free, loved, alive, righteous, sanctified, justified, and prosperous. Now why would you argue with that?!!!

It's time to step into the rhythm, get in the flow and let all your arguments go. You are My child! Don't argue anymore with the completed work, the work of redemption. Everything is included ... all things that pertain to life and godliness.

I chose you before the foundations of the earth. I handpicked you to do a work for ME!! Quit fussing and let's get moving. Night time is quickly approaching. We must build up My body. We'll get it done together. Can you contend with that? I'm ready! What about you? Stop being so confrontational! I desire to use you! You are My choice.

Mouth to mouth ... don't argue with me!

Prayer

Father, I am sorry for arguing with You. Thank You for choosing me to work alongside You. Today I accept the fact that I can be used by You, in Jesus' Name, Amen.

Prophetic Declaration

I declare that I am chosen by God to do extraordinary things. I decree it! It is so NOW, and so shall it be.

Notes

Day 31

..."Go in peace. Your journey has the Lord's approval."
Judges 18:6
New International Version

Journey:

an act of traveling from one place to another.

The Journey Begins Now

There is so much still left for us to do together. You are a partaker of My nature and an active participant of My work in the earth. The world is waiting on your arrival. The harvest is plenteous, yet those who labor are few. I have delivered you from bondage and the snares of the enemy for MY PLAN and MY USE!!

I know you thought it was over, but you've only just begun. I had you hidden in obscurity for a specific purpose. You were hidden away so you would not be caught up in the madness of people's opinions and the rationalization of who you should be. So many people thought that they were using you for their personal agendas ... I beg to differ. It was training ground where your faith muscles were being developed. What the enemy meant for your harm ... I have intercepted and already worked out for your good.

It was your belief in Me that kept you hopeful and has brought you to this point in your journey. I'm requiring more from you. Spontaneous living is what I need from you. You must rely on Me for every step. Trust Me. I have provided all you need. The people have already been selected to assist you.

You will have to stay close to Me for guidance, instructions, strategy, and moments of intimacy. It is on you to stay yielded and connected. Listen for Holy Spirit to whisper. You are going to be amazed at what I have prepared for you.

I am going to blow your mind. This is that which has been prophesied and what I've told you for years. It is the place where years of resistance becomes a pearl ... the place where, out of the darkness of the coals, a diamond is birthed ... a place where hidden riches and treasures are suddenly made available to you. This is the part of your journey where you get to reap from that which you have sown ... the part where the blessings overtake you ... the part of your journey in which I say it is evident that My hand is upon you.

Your critics will soon see that this point of your journey is all about Me and what I've done in you. Get moving ... your journey begins now. P.S. ... there is no need to take anything with you ... no cost either. At this point, it's all on Me.

Mouth the mouth ... begin your journey.

Prayer

Father, I thank You for this portion of my life's journey. I am here at Your bidding. Please make me ready for this part of my journey with You, in Jesus' Name, Amen.

Prophetic Declaration

I declare God's blessings are overtaking me today ... literally chasing me down. I decree and declare it. It is so NOW, and so shall it be.

Notes

Daily Rescue Breaths

(Appendix)

Day 1 ♥ Let Me Resuscitate You

Jesus said unto her, I am the resurrection, and the life: he that believeth on me, though he die, yet shall he live.
John 11:25
English Revised Version

I am severely afflicted; give me life, O Lord, according to your word.
Psalm 119:107
English Standard Version

Plead thou my cause, and redeem me: quicken me according to thy word.
Psalm 119:154
English Revised Version

For the sake of Your name, O Lord, revive me In Your righteousness bring my soul out of trouble.
Psalms 143:11
New American Standard

You who have shown me many troubles and distresses Will revive me again, And will bring me up again from the depths of the earth.
Psalm 71:20
New American Standard

Day 2 ♥ Intimacy Is Required

All things have been handed over to Me by My Father; and no one knows the Son except the Father; nor does anyone know the Father except the Son, and anyone to whom the Son wills to reveal Him.

Matthew 11:27
New American Standard

Abide in Me, and I in you. As the branch cannot bear fruit of itself unless it abides in the vine, so neither can you unless you abide in Me.
John 15.4
New American Standard

For [the Spirit which] you have now received [is] not a spirit of slavery to put you once more in bondage to fear, but you have received the Spirit of adoption [the Spirit producing sonship] in [the bliss of] which we cry, Abba (Father)! Father!
Romans 8:15
Amplified Bible

Greater love hath no man than this, that a man lay down his life for his friends.
John 15:13
American Standard Version

That I may know him, and the power of his resurrection, and the fellowship of his sufferings, being made conformable unto his death;
Philippians 3:10
King James Version

Day 3 ♥ I Am Winning You Back

Again, the kingdom of heaven is like a merchant seeking fine pearls, 46 and upon finding one pearl of great value, he went and sold all that he had and bought it.
Matthew 13:45-46
New American Standard

They heard the sound of the Lord God walking in the garden in the cool of the day ... Then the Lord God called to the man, and said to him, 'Where are you?'
Genesis 3:8-9
New American Standard

For thus says the Lord God: Behold, I Myself will search for My sheep and will seek them out.

Ezekiel 34:11
English Standard Version

... as a bridegroom rejoices over the bride, so your God will rejoice over you.
Isaiah 62:5
GOD'S WORD Translation

Then I passed by you and saw you, and behold, you were at the time for love; so I spread My skirt over you and covered your nakedness. I also swore to you and entered into a covenant with you so that you became Mine, declares the Lord.
Ezekiel 16:8
New King James Version

Day 4 ♥ I Am Wooing You!!!

"How priceless is your unfailing love! Both high and low among men find refuge in the shadow of your wings. They feast on the abundance of your house; you give them drink from your river of delights. For with you is the fountain of life; in your light we see light."
Psalm 36:7-9
New International Version

May the God of hope fill you with all joy and peace as you trust in him, so that you may overflow with hope by the power of the Holy Spirit.
Romans 15:13
New International Version

He brought me forth also into a large place; he delivered me, because he delighted in me.
Psalm 18:19
English Revised Version

In my distress I prayed to the LORD, and the LORD answered me and set me free.
Psalm 118:5

Father, I desire that they also, whom You have given Me, be with Me where I am …
John 17:24
New American Standard

Day 5 ♥ The Season for Suddenly

But the multitude of your enemies will become like fine dust, And the multitude of the ruthless ones like the chaff which blows away; And it will happen instantly, suddenly.
Isaiah 29:5
New American

"I foretold the former things long ago, My mouth announced them and I made them known; then suddenly I acted, and they came to pass."
Isaiah 48:3
New International Version

"You shall also decree a thing, and it shall be established for you: and the Light shall shine upon your ways,"
Job 22:28
King James 2000 Bible

"Son of man, behold, the house of Israel is saying, 'The vision that he sees is for many years from now, and he prophesies of times far off.' "Therefore say to them, 'Thus says the Lord GOD, "None of My words will be delayed any longer. Whatever word I speak will be performed,"' declares the Lord GOD,"
Ezekiel 12:27-28
New American Standard

"I would have despaired unless I had believed that I would see the goodness of the LORD In the land of the living. 14 Wait for the LORD; Be strong and let your heart take courage; Yes, wait for the LORD,"
Psalm 27:13.
New American Standard

Day 6 ♥ What Are You Seeking?

Seek the LORD and his strength, seek his face continually.
1 Chronicles 16:11
King James Version

Let all those that seek thee rejoice and be glad in thee: let such as love thy salvation say continually, The LORD be magnified.
Psalms 40:16
King James Version

But without faith [it is] impossible to please [him]: for he that cometh to God must believe that he is, and [that] he is a rewarder of them that diligently seek him.
Hebrews 11:6 -
New King James Version

And ye shall seek me, and find [me], when ye shall search for me with all your heart.
Jeremiah 29:13
King James Version

I love them that love me; and those that seek me early shall find me.
Proverbs 8:17
King James Version

Day 7 ♥ I Want to Use You

Who hath saved us, and called [us] with an holy calling, not according to our works, but according to his own purpose and grace, which was given us in Christ Jesus before the world began,
2 Timothy 1:9
King James Version

Being confident of this very thing, that he which hath begun a good work in you will perform [it] until the day of Jesus Christ:
Philippians 1:6
King James Version

For we are his workmanship, created in Christ Jesus for good works, which God afore prepared that we should walk in them.
Ephesians 2:10
English Revised Version

But for this very purpose have I let you live, that I might show you My power, and that My name may be declared throughout all the earth.
Exodus 9: 16
Amplified Bible

For I know the thoughts and plans that I have for you, says the Lord, thoughts and plans for welfare and peace and not for evil, to give you hope in your final outcome.
Jeremiah 29: 11
Amplified Bible

Day 8 ♥ I See You!

I will instruct you and teach you in the way which you should go; I will counsel you with My eye upon you.
Psalm 32:8
New American Standard

For His eyes are upon the ways of a man, And He sees all his steps.
Job 34:21
Darby Translation

"For the eyes of the Lord are toward the righteous, and his ears attend to their prayer, but the face of the Lord is against those who do evil.
1 Peter 3:12
New American Standard

But Noah found favor in the eyes of the LORD.
Genesis 6:8
New International

And no creature is hidden from his sight, but all are naked and exposed to the eyes of him to whom we must give account.
Hebrews 4:13
English Standard Version

Day 9 ♥ 911 – Draw Closer

How blessed is the one whom You choose and bring near to You To dwell in Your courts We will be satisfied with the goodness of Your house, Your holy temple.
Psalm 65:4
New American Standard

"For there will be a day when watchmen On the hills of Ephraim call out, 'Arise, and let us go up to Zion, To the LORD our God."
Jeremiah 31:6
New International Version

"Therefore say to them, 'Thus says the LORD of hosts, "Return to Me," declares the LORD of hosts, "that I may return to you," says the LORD of hosts.
Zechariah 1:3
New American Standard

Therefore, brethren, since we have confidence to enter the holy place by the blood of Jesus,
Hebrews 10:19
New American Standard

let us draw near to God with a sincere heart in full assurance of faith, having our hearts sprinkled to cleanse us from a guilty conscience and having our bodies washed with pure water.
Hebrews 10:22
Berean Study Bible

Day 10 ♥ I Want Total Control

Submit yourselves therefore to God. Resist the devil, and he will flee from you.
James 4:7
English Standard Version

I delight to do Your will, O my God; Your Law is within my heart.
Psalm 40:8
New American Standard

not by way of eye service, as men-pleasers, but as slaves of Christ, doing the will of God from the heart.
Ephesians 6:6
New American Standard

Your kingdom come Your will be done, on earth as it is in heaven.
Matthew 6:10
English Standard Version

And do not be conformed to this world, but be transformed by the renewing of your mind, so that you may prove what the will of God is, that which is good and acceptable and perfect.
Romans 12:2
New American Standard

Day 11 ♥ This Is The Time

but those who hope in the Lord will renew their strength. They will soar on wings like eagles; they will run and not grow weary, they will walk and not be faint
Isaiah 40:31
New International Version

There is a time for everything, and a season for every activity under the heavens
Ecclesiastes 3:1
New International Version

For the vision [is] yet for an appointed time, but at the end it shall speak, and not lie: though it tarry, wait for it; because it will surely come, it will not tarry.
Habakkuk 2:3
King James Version

For we are his workmanship, created in Christ Jesus unto good works, which God hath before ordained that we should walk in them.
Ephesians 2:10
King James Version

Wait on the LORD: be of good courage, and he shall strengthen thine heart: wait, I say, on the LORD.
Psalms 27:14
King James Version

Day 12 ♥ It Will Happen

Delight thyself also in the LORD; and he shall give thee the desires of thine heart.
Psalms 37:4
King James Version

The LORD will accomplish what concerns me; Your lovingkindness, O LORD, is everlasting; Do not forsake the works of Your hands.
Psalm 138:8
New American Standard

So will My word be which goes forth from My mouth; It will not return to Me empty, Without accomplishing what I desire, And without succeeding in the matter for which I sent it.
Isaiah 55:11
New American Standard

For those whom He foreknew, He also predestined to become conformed to the image of His Son, so that He would be the firstborn among many brethren;
Romans 8:29
New American Standard

so that no one would be disturbed by these afflictions; for you yourselves know that we have been destined for this.
1 Thessalonians 3:3
New American Standard

Day 13 ♥ Equipped To Serve

... fully equip you with every grace that you may need for the doing of His will, producing in us that which will truly please Him through Jesus Christ. To Him be the glory to the Ages of the Ages! Amen.
Hebrews 13:21
Weymouth New Testament

They equip God's servants so that they are completely prepared to do good things.
2 Timothy 3.17
GOD'S WORD® Translation

I can do everything through Him who gives me strength.
Philippians 4:13
New International Version

The LORD is my strength and my shield; my heart trusts in Him, and I am helped...
Psalm 28:7
Holman Christian Standard

The Spirit of the Lord GOD is upon me, Because the LORD has anointed me To bring good news to the afflicted; He has sent me to bind up the brokenhearted, To proclaim liberty to captives And freedom to prisoners;
Isaiah 61:1-2
New American Standard

For He whom God has sent speaks the words of God; for He gives the Spirit without measure.
John 3:34
New American Standard

Day 14 ♥ Pursue It Regardless

And Jesus said to them, "Follow Me, and I will make you become fishers of men."
Mark 1:17
Lexham English Bible

And He called the twelve together, and gave them power and authority over all the demons and to heal diseases.
Luke 9:1-2
New American Standard

But to each one is given the manifestation of the Spirit for the common good.
1 Corinthians 12:7
New American Standard

Fight the good fight of faith; take hold of the eternal life to which you were called, and you made the good confession in the presence of many witnesses.
1 Timothy 6:12
New American Standard

So we have the prophetic word made more sure, to which you do well to pay attention as to a lamp shining in a dark place, until the day dawns and the morning star arises in your hearts.
2 Peter 1:19
New American Standard

Day 15 ♥ It's Right

For unto whosoever much is given, of him shall much be required
Luke 12:48, KJV
King James Version

Faithful is he that calleth you, who also will do it
1 Thessalonians 5:24
King James Bible

But let patience have [her] perfect work, that ye may be perfect and entire, wanting nothing
James 1:4
King James Bible

Being filled with the fruits of righteousness, which are by Jesus Christ, unto the glory and praise of God.
Philippians 1:11
Jubilee Bible 2000

"But the anointing that you received from him abides in you, and you have no need that anyone should teach you. But as his anointing teaches you about everything, and is true, and is no lie—just as it has taught you, abide in him."
1 John 2:27
English Standard Version

Day 16 ♥ It's All Up To You!

I will go before thee, and make the crooked places straight: I will break in pieces the gates of brass, and cut in sunder the bars of iron:
Isaiah 45:2
King James Bible

Every valley shall be filled, and every mountain and hill shall be brought low; and the crooked shall be made straight, and the rough ways shall be made smooth;
Luke 3:5
King James Bible

... in whom we have boldness and confident access through faith in Him.
Ephesians 3:12
King James Bible

He that saith he abideth in him ought himself.
I John 2:6
King James Bible

"I tell you the truth, anyone who believes in me will do the same works I have done, and even greater works, because I am going to be with the Father.
John 14:12
New Living Translation

Day 17 ♥ Surely I Will Lead You

For as many as are led by the Spirit of God, they are the sons of God.
Romans 8:14
King James Bible

... for a wide door for effective work has opened to me, and there are many adversaries.
1 Corinthians 16:8-9
King James Bible

I am the door. If anyone enters by me, he will be saved and will go in and out and find pasture.
John 10:9
English Standard Version (ESV)

"Then I will set the key of the house of David on his shoulder, When he opens no one will shut, When he shuts no one will open.
Isaiah 22:22
New American Standard

Now when I came to Troas for the gospel of Christ and when a door was opened for me in the Lord ...
2 Corinthians 2:12
New American Standard

Day 18 ♥ Pushed Into Your Assignment

I know how to be brought low, and I know how to abound. In any and every circumstance, I have learned the secret of facing plenty and hunger, abundance and need. I can do all things through him who strengthens me.
Philippians 4:12-13
English Standard Version

If you faint in the day of adversity, your strength is small.
Proverbs 24:10
English Standard Version

Have I not commanded you? Be strong and courageous. Do not be frightened, and do not be dismayed, for the Lord is with you wherever you go."
Joshua 1:9
English Standard Version

But you, take courage! Do not let your hands be weak, for your work shall be rewarded."
2 Chronicles 15:7
English Standard Version

Beloved, do not be surprised at the fiery trial when it comes upon you to test you, as though something strange were happening to you. But rejoice insofar as you share Christ's sufferings, that you may also rejoice and be glad when his glory is revealed.
1 Peter 4:12-13
ESV

Day 19 ♥ Open Doors That NO MAN Can Close!!!!

"And to the angel of the church in Philadelphia write: 'The words of the holy one, the true one, who has the key of David, who opens and no one will shut, who shuts and no one opens.
Revelation 3:7
ESV

They arrested the apostles and put them in the public prison. But during the night an angel of the Lord opened the prison doors and brought them out,

and said, "Go and stand in the temple and speak to the people all the words of this Life."
Acts 5:18-20
ESV

saying, "We found the prison house locked quite securely and the guards standing at the doors; but when we had opened up, we found no one inside.
Acts 5:23
New American Standard

So if the Son sets you free, you will be free indeed.
John 8:36
English Standard Version

For you meet him with rich blessings; you set a crown of fine gold upon his head.
Psalm 21:3
English Standard Version

Day 20 ♥ Labor To Rest

"My presence will go with you, and I will give you rest."
Exodus 33:14
New International Version

"My soul finds rest in God alone; my salvation comes from him. He alone is my rock and my salvation; he is my fortress, I will never be shaken."
Psalm 62:1-2
New International Version

"Let us therefore strive to enter that rest, so that no one may fall by the same sort of disobedience."
Hebrews 4:11
English Standard Version

"Unless the Lord builds the house, those who build it labor in vain. Unless the Lord guards the city, the guard keeps watch in vain. It is in vain that you

rise up early and go late to rest, eating the bread of anxious toil; for he gives sleep to his beloved."
Psalm 127: 1-2
New Revised Standard Version

"Be anxious for nothing, but in everything by prayer and supplication with thanksgiving let your requests be made known to God. And the peace of God, which surpasses all comprehension, shall guard your hearts and your minds in Christ Jesus."
Philippians 4: 6-7
New American Standard Version

Day 21 ♥ Open Your Mouth

For the word of God [is] quick, and powerful, and sharper than any two-edged sword, piercing even to the dividing asunder of soul and spirit, and of the joints and marrow, and [is] a discerner of the thoughts and intents of the heart.
Hebrews 4:12
King James Bible

All scripture [is] given by inspiration of God, and [is] profitable for doctrine, for reproof, for correction, for instruction in righteousness:...
2 Timothy 3:16-17 -
King James Bible

Do you have the gift of speaking? Then speak as though God himself were speaking through you. Do you have the gift of helping others? Do it with all the strength and energy that God supplies. Then everything you do will bring glory to God through Jesus Christ. All glory and power to him forever and ever! Amen.
1 Peter 4:11
New Living Translation

He who hears you hears me..."
Luke 10:16a
New King James Version

"I am the LORD your God, who brought you out of the land of Egypt; open your mouth wide, and I will fill it."
Psalm 81:1
New International Version

Day 22 ♥ What Is Your Passion?

My soul longs, yes, faints for the courts of the Lord; my heart and flesh sing for joy to the living God.
Psalm 84:2
ESV

Complete my joy by being of the same mind, having the same love, being in full accord and of one mind.
Philippians 2:2
ESV

Set me as a seal upon your heart, as a seal upon your arm, for love is strong as death, jealousy is fierce as the grave. Its flashes are flashes of fire, the very flame of the Lord. Many waters cannot quench love, neither can floods drown it. If a man offered for love all the wealth of his house, he would be utterly despised.
Song of Solomon 8:6-7
ESV

As a deer pants for streams, so pants my soul for you, O God.
Psalm 42:1
ESV

Look carefully then how you walk! Live purposefully and worthily and accurately, not as the unwise and witless, but as wise (sensible, intelligent people).
Ephesians 5: 15
Amplified Bible

Day 23 ♥ Release Your Faith

"For all the promises of God in him are yes, and in him Amen, unto the glory of God by us."
2 Corinthians 1:20
New King James Version

I had fainted, unless I had believed to see the goodness of the LORD in the land of the living.
Psalm 27:13
King James Bible

... For therein is the righteousness of God revealed from faith to faith: as it is written, The just shall live by faith.
Romans 1:17
King James Bible

"Through faith we understand that the worlds were framed by the word of God, so that things which are seen were <u>not</u> made of things which do appear."
Hebrews 11:3
King James Bible

But Jesus told him, "No! The Scriptures say, 'People do not live by bread alone, but by every word that comes from the mouth of God.'"
Matthew 4:4
New Living Translation

Day 24 ♥ My Prophetic Expression

So God created man in his own image, in the image of God he created him; male and female he created them.
Genesis 1:27
English Standard Version

Surely the Lord GOD will do nothing, but he revealeth his secret unto his servants the prophets.

Amos 3:7
King James Bible

For the prophecy came not in old time by the will of man: but holy men of God spake [as they were] moved by the Holy Ghost.
2 Peter 1:21
King James Bible

Have I not commanded you? Be strong and courageous. Do not be frightened, and do not be dismayed, for the Lord your God is with you wherever you go."
Joshua 1:9
English Standard Version

Do not be anxious about anything, but in everything by prayer and supplication with thanksgiving let your requests be made known to God. And the peace of God, which surpasses all understanding, will guard your hearts and your minds in Christ Jesus.
Philippians 4:6-7
English Standard Version

Day 25 ♥ Let Me Do It

The steps of a man are established by the LORD, when he delights in his way;
Psalm 37:23
English Standard Version

Your word is a lamp to my feet and a light to my path.
Psalm 119:105
English Standard Version

And your ears shall hear a word behind you, saying, "This is the way, walk in it," when you turn to the right or when you turn to the left.
Isaiah 30:21
English Standard Version

And the LORD will guide you continually and satisfy your desire in scorched places and make your bones strong; and you shall be like a watered garden, like a spring of water, whose waters do not fail.

Isaiah 58:11
English Standard Version

If anyone's will is to do God's will, he will know whether the teaching is from God or whether I am speaking on my own authority.

John 7:17
English Standard Version

Day 26 ♥ What Is Your Role?

But ye [are] a chosen generation, a royal priesthood, an holy nation, a peculiar people; that ye should shew forth the praises of him who hath called you out of darkness into his marvelous light:

1 Peter 2:9
King James Version

For we are his workmanship, created in Christ Jesus unto good works, which God hath before ordained that we should walk in them.

Ephesians 2:10
King James Bible

Ye are of God, little children, and have overcome them: because greater is he that is in you, than he that is in the world.

1 John 4:4
King James Bible

I praise you, for I am fearfully and wonderfully made. Wonderful are your works; my soul knows it very well.

Psalm 139:14
English Standard Version

Put on then, as God's chosen ones, holy and beloved, compassionate hearts, kindness, humility, meekness, and patience,

Colossians 3:12

He has delivered us from the domain of darkness and transferred us to the kingdom of his beloved Son,
Colossians 1:13
English Standard Version

Day 27 ♥ Finished Business

"If you are faithful in little things, you will be faithful in large ones. But if you are dishonest in little things, you won't be honest with greater responsibilities."
Luke 16:10
New Living Translation

"Unless the Lord builds the house, the builders labor in vain."
Psalm 127:1
New International Version

Commit to the Lord whatever you do, and he will establish your plans.
Proverbs 16:3
New International Version

And they overcame him by the blood of the Lamb, and by the word of their testimony; and they loved not their lives unto the death.
Revelation 12:11
King James Version

And He sent them out to proclaim the kingdom of God and to perform healing.
Luke 9:2
New American Standard

Day 28 ♥ I Have A Need

My God will richly fill your every need in a glorious way through Christ Jesus.
Philippians 4:19
GOD'S WORD® Translation

Jesus said to her, "Did I not tell you that if you believed you would see the glory of God?"
John 11:40
English Standard Version

No weapon that is fashioned against you shall succeed, and you shall refute every tongue that rises against you in judgment. This is the heritage of the servants of the LORD and their vindication from me, declares the LORD."
Isaiah 54:17
English Standard Version

And we know that for those who love God all things work together for good, for those who are called according to his purpose.
Romans 8:28
English Standard Version

But overhearing what they said, Jesus said to the ruler of the synagogue, "Do not fear, only believe."
Mark 5:36
English Standard Version

Day 29 ♥ You Have To Want It!

You will seek me and find me, when you seek me with all your heart.
Jeremiah 29:13
English Standard Version

Yes, if you call out for insight and raise your voice for understanding, if you seek it like silver and search for it as for hidden treasures, then you will understand the fear of the Lord And find the knowledge of God.
Proverbs 2:3-5
English Standard Version

But they who wait for the Lord shall renew their strength; they shall mount up with wings like eagles; they shall run and not be weary; they shall walk and not faint.
Isaiah 40:31
English Standard Version

Not that I have already obtained this or am already perfect, but I press on to make it my own, because Christ Jesus has made me his own. Brothers, I do not consider that I have made it my own. But one thing I do: forgetting what lies behind and straining forward to what lies ahead, I press on toward the goal for the prize of the upward call of God in Christ Jesus.
Philippians 3:12-14
English Standard Version

For it is God who works in you, both to will and to work for his good pleasure.
Philippians 2:13
English Standard Version

Day 30 ♥ Don't Argue with Me!

I am my beloved's, and his desire is for me.
Song of Solomon 7:10
English Standard Version

You did not choose me, but I chose you and appointed you that you should go and bear fruit and that your fruit should abide, so that whatever you ask the Father in my name, he may give it to you.
John 15:16
English Standard Version

"Before I formed you in the womb I knew you, and before you were born I consecrated you; I appointed you a prophet to the nations."
Jeremiah 1:5
English Standard Version

"For God so loved the world, that he gave his only Son, that whoever believes in him should not perish but have eternal life."
John 3:16
English Standard Version

But the anointing that you received from him abides in you, and you have no need that anyone should teach you. But as his anointing teaches you about everything, and is true, and is no lie—just as it has taught you, abide in him.
1 John 2:27
English Standard Version

Day 31 ♥ The Journey Begins Now

Behold, I am doing a new thing; now it springs forth, do you not perceive it? I will make a way in the wilderness and rivers in the desert.
Isaiah 43:19
ESV

The steadfast love of the Lord never ceases; his mercies never come to an end; they are new every morning; great is your faithfulness. "The Lord is my portion," says my soul, "therefore I will hope in Him."
Lamentations 3:22-24
ESV

And though your beginning was small, your latter days will be very great.
Job 8:7
ESV

And let us not grow weary of doing good, for in due season we will reap, if we do not give up.
Galatians 6:9
English Standard Version